*Uncertain Grace*

# Uncertain Grace

*Rebecca Liv Wee*

COPPER CANYON PRESS

Cover art: *Maize and Cockscomb,* Japanese, six-fold screen (detail); colors on gold leaf on paper, Edo period, mid-seventeenth century, Kate S. Buckingham Fund, 1959.599 overall. Photograph by Robert Hashimoto. Photograph © 2000, The Art Institute of Chicago, all rights reserved.

Copper Canyon Press is in residence under the auspices of the Centrum Foundation at Fort Worden State Park in Port Townsend, Washington. Centrum sponsors artist residencies, education workshops for Washington State students and teachers, blues, jazz, and fiddle tunes festivals, classical music performances, and The Port Townsend Writers' Conference.

LIBRARY OF CONGRESS CATALOGING-IN-PUBLICATION DATA

Wee, Rebecca Liv, 1962–
Uncertain grace / Rebecca Liv Wee.
    p.  cm.
ISBN 1-55659-154-3 (alk. paper)
1. Title.
PS3623 E4 U53 2001
811'.6 — DC21                                        2001002046


9 8 7 6 5 4 3 2 FIRST EDITION
COPPER CANYON PRESS
Post Office Box 271
Port Townsend, Washington 98368
www.coppercanyonpress.org

For you, Michael.

Muscles better and nerves more.

2000 HAYDEN CARRUTH AWARD

The Hayden Carruth Award was established in 1998 to honor the most distinguished first, second, or third book manuscript from among more than one thousand annual entries received at Copper Canyon Press.

ACKNOWLEDGMENTS

Poems in this collection have appeared in the following journals:

*The Iowa Review*
*The Mid-America Poetry Review*
*the minnesota review*
*Phoebe*
*Ploughshares*
*The Plum Review*
*Rag Mag*
*The Sonora Review*

I am grateful to the editors, and to the Minnesota State Arts Board for a 1994 fellowship grant which provided time to work on these poems. Thanks go also to Sam Hamill, Michael Wiegers, Jane Miller, and friends at Copper Canyon Press.

I am indebted to the poets whose example, wisdom, and care have fed me — Carolyn Forché, Donald Hall, and Karen Herseth Wee especially.

Michael Hudson has my love and gratitude for inspiring new work, for his fierce confidence and support, and for bringing me such happiness.

The most beautiful thoughts are shadows.

PAUL VALÉRY

I could be undone every single day by
paradox or what they call in the countryside
blackthorn winter....

EAVAN BOLAND

# Contents

*Uncertain Grace*

# PART ONE

# The Philosopher

A man rides a bicycle into town. He's forgotten his clothes,
or maybe this is what he means to do.
He rides carefully into the burning town.

Apartments of old stone list, iron balconies, awnings,
the window-grates blacken with heat. He rides by.

His lip perspires, his eyes intent.
In the hills behind him there is a glow that is not the burning.
The Acropolis maybe. The Dome of the Rock.

The man has a book under his arm. The pages are gilt-edged, the title
has worn away. He has a shoulder-wound also, an old crescent scar.
Now his chest sweats, now his abdomen.
He is more agile than laughter.

The road turns. A black sedan rounds the corner
behind him. They are leaving town or they're trailing him.
Either way it's too late.

The man is not cold without clothes. He sees whole worlds
wherever he looks, and this keeps him busy.
Maps and globes and civilizations not on fire.

Now when he stops and considers the spokes, the bicycle tires,
he sees ashes, nails, explosions of glass.

He does not believe in this. He believes in something else.

# Beyond Preemption, Illinois

It's possible there was no bridge painted teal,
rust coming through like bruising

Or that when I stepped from the gravel road
into the ditch of timothy and scattered glass there was no applause,
no commentary from the cornfields, each stalk rustling,
silk and husks

And that snake wrapped around the top strand of barbed wire—
it's possible, I suppose, that it got there itself

That what appeared to be greying cord
        —half-stiffened, half-paper, its finished life
        flaking off in the sun—

                                had been a cadence, a taproot

Such things may not matter

It may be gone when I look for it next, brought down by rain,
bird-pecked

I might begin to believe I imagined it

It's possible the world keeps its horrors largely to itself
in spite of what we read, what we know

And the child's wagon down there in the creekbed,
overturned, one side shot through, in the pokeweed—

I suppose it might not be anything, after all

# Still Life

In black and white the pear turns to iron,

cold in the light, its stem a dark bone

Something from a märchen where there are reasons

for still, beautiful things

Elaborate spells spun around artifacts—jeweled combs,

spindles, pieces of fruit, a thing on a table

Until one day the least likely peasant in his ragged blouse

sees it fixed in winter light and knows

he must feel the metal in his palms, must press

the fruit to his lips where it becomes a woman or a swan

Something muscular, supple

The scent of blood and rain rushing in

# *hoop snake*

Any of several snakes, such as the mud snake, said to grasp the tail in
the mouth and move with a rolling, hooplike motion.

AMERICAN HERITAGE DICTIONARY OF THE
ENGLISH LANGUAGE

the second time we met
he told me about the hoop snake

(temporal, exquisite,
a godless man

so I listened)

we weren't sure though
if it could be true

a snake that takes its tail in its mouth,
then rolls through the world

but there are reasons to believe in god
and this seems a good one

we brought wine to the porch, spoke
of piety, marriage,

devotion assumed for reasons
that could not sustain it

while lightning took apart the sky
the fields leapt up the stream's

muddy lustre its sinuous length
liminal, lush, the grass black

the unheard melodies and those that catch
the leaves beginning to fret

I don't remember now what he said his eyes
revising that dark

after he left I walked through the grass the rain
asked *how do things work?*

we are after something miraculous

we open our mouths we believe
we turn
at times

we gather speed

# Red Tide

Memory insists on the press of his mouth. Winter grapes in a bowl,
        a blanket.

No moon as he knelt at the fire pit, his beauty amplified, briefly fixed
while beyond him the breakers' blue lava poured from the crest of each
        next collapse.

Fusion of fates. Some turbulent grace cast into motion,
gesture, sand and waves, the voluptuous reassembling of the shore.

And in those instants, the waves' dark cargo —
secrets in the drag and suck. Filigree of beachtrash.

What I know is despotic desire: for his voice, his hands, the logs' hiss
        and snap.
That kite snagged at the top of a palm.

That he took us there then — a prompt from the gods, a tease, our
        dumb luck.
Once every thirty years, we were told, a night like that

when what looks like coral or rust in the day-waves turns numinous in
        the dark.
Blue surge and lunge, that harrowing pull, shot through with banquets
        of light.

The woman I was walking into it.

# Chiroptera

The walk home is later and so it happens
in darker light. Such a wind on the face,

on the glamorous graveyard, the city
with its bronze horses and their men,

and the white stone shrines light up
at night. The air is less supple,

less fecund here. The bats are out.

In Bangalore sandalwood incense
dropped its small heaps of ash. We sat

beneath netting, unhinged in sweat,
smoking slim sweet-rolled leaves.

Each night low-pitched whistles
came from the well, then suddenly

there at the screen, tapping canes
as watchmen prowled the grounds,

flushing out cobras, ducking bats
big as geese. A cat leaps

from a neighbor's shrub, a black flash,
and I flinch, almost run. Leaves click

on branches, they scrape against trunks
and gutters, hollowish, no more green

in the sound. Something flaps
on a low limb, I spin left. Nothing

after all, but still it comes on,
an enormous fluttering

tree. We noticed it because everything else
on the street hung so still.

How could the great dark leaves be stirring,

what breeze had we missed?

# *Thought*

*La pensée se fait dans la bouche*
TRISTAN TZARA

I wake after fields

After sun

Stuttering
On the earth's far curve

And the thought of it —

(Rousing you

Troubling the leaves
The winter spinach gone wild)

Suddenly it comes again

In the light firing your hair, your eyes

But I've not said
I love you, you don't know

How I've traveled the spirals
Along some edge
Of your perception

How in still moments, in quiet, I am
A hiss, a phrasing of hands

An arched brown foot

And the unsaid

Scorched fields

# Heart's Itch

*a few blossoms, the lowly mountains, that pair in the tunnel of love*
*— and it is a tunnel, and it is love —*

JANE MILLER

We walked, undressed, in a tawny field, and the heat
on my legs where the sun hit, dear god, your voice reeling into my ear.
I believe in a source, I do. A soul.

A reason, however unsound. Even nostalgia and its distortions —
in spite of the unmarked graves.

Later, fire-vine stitched over stucco, apples on a white plate,
a freezer clacking with ice.

There *is* something to it, something creaturely, raw,
in the stretch of your spine. Your dear lips.

Tonight fog takes the ravine. An owl amends the quiet.

On a beach a man pushes a cart with his life
through the sand. A shoe, a towel, the tinging of cans.

The moon that scores his face perfects yours.
What are we to make of this?
The sky is filling with black flowers.

Still, love insists on the ludicrous: nicknames, kissing in the street.

My darling, what is it, this mulish faith that wheels and gleams
between us? A trace of headway? Recovery from loss?
That pair of hawks overhead?

# Uncertain Grace

*after Sebastião Salgado*

How can she be beautiful? Eyes, ribs, the slope
and angle of bone. The flesh itself is finished,
so close it's come to the end

of hunger, a husk set aside, tied
at the knees and ankles. Thumbs hooked
with clean white cord. What used to be.

Famine in the Sahel, the eyes blown out.

She graces and wrecks the gallery walls
with her vanishing. Her lips dark with flies.

A man stubs out his cigarette.

⌁

And still the earth's haunches, its flanks of sand.
Devious leaves and riverbeds, the pungent stars.

Something petaled and lush near the stone tomb
where her eyes may yet open.

Swept clean. Someone has left a plate of salt fish
and wine. This is arousal — how things live sometimes
beyond great hurt. Elastic beauty. The lunatic flesh.

# PART TWO

# Crossings

Streetlamps in March, headlights turned
on the realization in '64

that apparently altruistic traits in species
could be versions of light on water. Motion

passing through New York City, its wounded
impaired for the rest of their lives. Long-reaching

steps from one to the next. Each of us
on a toehold, on curious rocks

in streams with our new blood
spent. Think of Verrazano Bridge. The longest

suspension bridge in the world opened
to traffic. A voice saying *Careful. Don't fall in.*

So there's caution.
Light. Always arms being held straight up

in the air. Harry Harlow showing how monkeys
reared in isolation suffer

severe emotional impairment. We cross
on pebbles worn flat, try to stand

in the midst and above the rushing.
Like glittering ragged snow. The same

plasmid that carries resistance to penicillin
in staphylococci

permits the bacteria that possess the plasmid
to survive a mercury-based variety

of normally toxic metals. Venus and Saturn
cross streams with their arms up. Artemis

falling in brilliance. A raindrop, a tin flame,
headlights on ice. We learn the mathematics

of Mendelian heredity (peas in the monastery
garden), but don't yet understand impairment.

How a great earthquake shook Alaska, how
the International Year of the Quiet Sun begins.

# Ajabu

ajabu *is a Swahili word for "magical"*

Kenyan stamps on blue tissue—the usual pregnant arrival of words.
Always a marvel with facts and specifics, she notices things

no one else notices, then shares them with a practical generosity.
*You might as well know this.*

And after she says she's grown fat on chocolate, outlines a day
of clinical work and tells of a hippo, the green mambas in the yard,

there is something else. A woman in labor. Undilated and staring
into the eyes of something, she arrived alone from the village.

No supplies in the cabinets, no time and two hours of one ruptured dirt road.
They carried her to the Jeep, knew they'd never make Migori before she collapsed,

then *how stunned we were to find the road repaired!* The ruts filled in, tangled
roots and rock removed, smoothed over. They made it in forty-five minutes,

delivered the woman and her child and afterward asked when the road was restored,
how, by whom. Why had they heard no shovels, no singing?

The nurses shook their heads then, the hagglers in the market shrugged. At dusk
they turned the Jeep for home, lurched back onto the road and *you must know this—*

She writes of the endless ragged tracks, the old sprawling scar, and how for two hours
in silence they labored their way back, each star beating down.

# Graffiti under Memorial Bridge

⤙

Often I remind myself that things are charged.

    I can hear Howard—
    "I've leant my bike up against that little bush. It will be
              perfectly all right
    if no one touches it."

Someone touches it.

⤙

In a grim niche squats a grotesque stone. It's the Ape of Thoth lit weirdly
from above by the day filtering through red glass.

One block down they shake Styrofoam cups, ask the air and its
       coatsleeves for coins.

⤙

    (If God seems removed from the immediacy of human events, well,
    as a baby He was found in a handbag in Victoria Station.)

I have been asking you to explain a few things and still what I hear
       are echoes.

It could be that we've failed.

⤙

"In one hundred years we shall be the same age,"
says Anna McDaniels. "But I live in a city of walls, all kinds,

and they are almost all I know."

⤳

In places where violence stifles daylight
and bulbs grow soft with neglect,

fungal delicacy must be dug from the ground.

In Maine a janitor goes to jail for harvesting hemp in his backyard.
Six years.

⤳

Turning off the television is easily done but our mental turmoil
must be watched. What sex are we? How do we know?

The world is covered with people who are watching events.
Frankly, they get in the way.

⤳

At some point in the evening, a haggard young man always bounds onstage
to announce that he is Hamlet's ghost. His posture is right, the lights drop
to red—

a horrid ache. Smoke in the lobby.

The rising portamento.

ᨤ

We learn there is no elegant history. The news reminds us
that things are charged.

"Four o'clock. My poor cats.
What a bore for them if humanity has to be saved
every afternoon."

ᨤ

Father: donning a white apron.
Madame: with her penchant for certain combinations of blue and yellow.

# Baudelaire to His Mother

Shall I bring the chateaubriand or will you wait?
Your letters have been full of the most frightful things;
I shall never get used to them. And here I am,
wandering about with my shawl. The material is lovely
but the antiquity of the design is an invincible obstacle
to its sale.

I must make a lot of money to escape from Paris.
I have neither the courage nor the genius
of Balzac, yet I have all the complications
that made him so wretched. You see, dear Mother,
I am in a fairly grave condition for a man
whose profession is to produce and clothe
creatures of the imagination.

The right leg is swollen, and cannot be bent and the pain
is exceedingly strange; some say it is cramp, others neuralgia.
Opium has terrible inconveniences.
But *come at once,* you say.

Do I need a change of air? I cannot tell. Is it my sick body
that weakens my will and mind or is it
a spiritual cowardice wears out my body?
I beg you not to send me phrases
such as these: *To speak truly — Charles, you made me despair!* or
*A careful man has always enough money by him to meet such things.*

REFUSE ME SIMPLY, OR SEND THE MONEY.

I have an intolerable fear of poverty.

What I feel is an immense discouragement, a sensation of
unbearable isolation, a perpetual fear of some remote disaster,

an utter disbelief in my capacity,

a total absence of desire.

An impossibility of finding any kind of interest.

The strange success of my book
and the hatred it roused interested me for a little,
but afterwards I fell back again.

I send you some articles printed about *Les Fleurs du mal,*
by various nobodies. But my abominable existence
and brandy, which I am going to stop, have impaired my stomach
these last months, and besides,
I have nervous crises, exactly like a woman.

REFUSE ME SIMPLY, OR SEND THE MONEY.

Obsessed by moments of longing to sleep eternally, yet now
I cannot sleep at all, my mind is so busy. Why should I add
that I went through the winter fireless?
It is too stupid.

I scrawl most fearfully.

My clothes are quite adequate. The fifty francs (!)
are maternal, but the handkerchiefs are a stroke of genius.

I am in a pitiable state of mind and body; so bad
that I envy everyone. If ever a man were ill with an illness
medicine cannot cure, I am that man.

I have an intolerable fear of poverty though my clothes
are quite adequate.

I ask myself unceasingly: what is the good of this?
Accursed festivals reminding us of the flight of time;
how badly we use it; how full of sorrow it is.

I am riddled with affairs and worries. I do not refer to them
as that would hurt you unnecessarily.

I scrawl most fearfully.

Do you want your chateaubriand now or will you wait?

# Mount Pleasant Hydrangea

Opened the door to find no one
who might have knocked
but instead blue flowers
hang heavy and obscene
from stalks
bent over the walk

Not aquamarine, not azure

not even sky blue
but blue like the rims of stained carnations, the sharp blue

of plastic shovels and pails
for the beach
like a notebook
with a blue cover, the blue caps
of pens

And these are the petals and these the blue
stems that grow in my rooms

At dinner suddenly they push up
through the floor

though the guests don't see how their legs are being wrapped
in leaves, how the great blue blooms
have reached their napkined laps
the cool bowls of soup

When we walk the streets
no one sees the flowers
filling the children's mouths

The men lounging on storefront steps
don't feel the blue anthers moving up through
their pockets

There are stamens in the eaves, porches
and birdbaths overrun

pollen spilling from tailpipes
indigo pavement, cerulean lawns

Blue mist in the rooms where tea steeps

Where veins like blue roots make their way through us
to blossom, to vigorous rot

# After Trakl's "Autumn Evening"

She agrees with autumn prowling the walls.
The tobacco clouds convene and brood—
she says they add scent and help the brown village
limp to the edge of the picture.

What she can't see are the dead.

She wants to know if the man is married to the wife,
she supposes it's a very small village,
breathlessly close with its red earth
and soot, its shadows smudged into stairwells.
Pressed into deep corners of things.

She says if there is a tavern in town
there is loneliness also, cork boots
kicking up dust and the sounds of loss
strung out as laughter in public places.
The girls she's not interested in.

Boys and cesspools, those she can see,
but *moist blueness?* If that's what the girls are about,
then she says they are blind to the shadows

and it's shadows that count in the end.
Shadows are what hold everything together,
she whispers, and those girls

stepping quickly over the drunks don't see
the crux. The slurring. The wild birds.

# Pont des Arts

She's bent in a posture of anguish or prayer
in a spot of city filth.

Head down, a stained knit cap
with its few coins on the ground beside her,
and her pliant child, a shadow.

Someone veers past with a friend
in a clamor of rings and scarves. A pretty child
skips after them, scattering pigeons.

The mothers miss how their daughters' eyes catch then —
the wary, openmouthed stares.

A terrible knowledge passes between them,
the bridge rippling under their feet

as the polished child rushes past but looks back
at the one on the bridge in the heat —

the sunblown silent one
whose hand has pulled back and flown up to smooth,
for a moment, her heavy hair.

# Intarsia

Next door a child shifts in sleep. Cats crouch in the roses.
There's a man walking coatless through dark rain

and the days fill with such ordinary strangeness that taking the
          garbage out
hurts. I have grown afraid of reflection,

of both silence and squalls, of being
alone in this.

There's a boy in Rome
whose eyes broke me, a Thai woman still bringing poppies in

from the fields. In Jerusalem a madman wears my watch.
There are canaries hanging in doorways in cages

and from the Mount of Olives
such sweeps of cypress and white stone.

Steam under surfaces, goats on roofs.

Thin-legged boys hock strands of shells. At Cape Comorin
the salt of three seas comes together.
An old man wrapped in yellow waits on the rocks.

The child next door is asleep in Cochin. The coatless man stands
          begging for coins
in Bombay, his shirt of lace

sparkles where it's held together with bits of wire, tiny pins.

# St. Johanns Spital, Salzburg

*Hematology, March 17, 1997*

we wait for good news from the hall of green doors
on this day of rain the streets smell of herring the Salzach's gulls
blow like paper scraps

finally they have called him in
a poster of spiny white flowers shivers in a crosswind from another hall

we're among the last here idiot *Ausländer* it took us hours to understand
there are no appointments just lines of waiting a girl with black eyes
kicks her chair bites her lip glares into the nurses' backs

I've begun to expect not to speak be addressed
the words don't assemble my tongue sticks a curious din in my ears

the flowers shudder against the door

he's grown so thin he fades beneath me inside a shadow
still we came here it rains the sky bearing down

all weekend I watched us my aerial view a calm that could break
into dread or sift yet toward safety his blood was never so big

the waiting room plants thrive the toilets are broken
a vending machine spits back each coin
in a corner a child invents her life with three chairs her shiny red purse

she narrates with arcs with delicate poise she whispers into the air

there's a woman whose robe gapes her breasts are monstrous her leg
bandaged ankle to thigh she makes telephone calls for an hour

when a nurse slips in I see him my darling the stepping-stones
of the spine I love dressed or otherwise gentle or not
with him at last how I am in a room is easy it fits

how I clean or weep when I wake

later he'll say they took marrow he'll tell me how they pulled it from
        his sternum
sent him back to the hall where I'll hate that they don't know
his hands his mind how carefully they work

the girl with illness about her eyes comes back through one of the doors
I can't read her look of surprise her hand twitches over her heart

she walks off into a short or long life I hear her feet all the way down
        the hall

# PART THREE

# After the Crazy Mountains

Marigolds in the breakfast eggs
A bottle of green light a sill
Something liminal
The road sighs spits
Gravel flashing with glass
Heat lightning
Apache tears
His voice lurching through
Phone lines over borders
Ninety degrees in a room in Butte
The carpet audibly green
An eighty-ton steel Madonna
On the Continental Divide
Marlboro in the towels the sheets
On a wall "Anaconda Meat"
Signs for Tongue River,
Browse, Silt, and No Name
"A woman traveling across
the plains with a wagon train
of emigrants went insane"
Exhaust exhalations dropped
Like gauze from a plane
The migrant workers
Bright shirts bent flowers
They stoop through it their backs
Dusted fruit trucks of beets
At dusk a man crosses a street
Fingers on the clumped throats
Of poppies stems their roots
Sweep the asphalt the country

Is stitched with fenceline
Quiet reminders a crow's eye
The fleck of light it carries
Words in a book
Worn with touch with desire
The lick and shock of
His voice every town
again
again
NOTE: *learn to notice*
*what you notice*
The heated wood of a bench
This syllable tendency stance
Velvet light
A horse vanishing into a canyon
Rest-stop filth faucets tile
"She escaped from the party
and was found near these mountains"
A car buried to its gone windows
In thistle in restless grass
The goldenrod brutally yellow
NOTE: *your vocation is to be faithful*
All night the threnody of trains
Their keening and scream
The cry after something breaks
A heart pulled past bearing
His voice silicate vertical
A flower that looks
Like a paintbrush upended
As if it had been touched

To crimson then poised
At the trail's edge
*You must act*
*as if the truth were true*

# Nebraska

*watch for wind on overpass*

a tremor of air at the crest, then
the fields, the shoulder

from which it would be so easy
to fall. be blown. we had been feeling anyway

like paper scraps.
the wind the previous day

thickets of rain, something cold and blue
in a glass

cornstalks, clouds flapping

the green, the battered earth.
asphalt

then one of us on the shoulder
head down

walking off as the light collapses

becomes a thunder moon.
a partially burnt-out neon sign
reads VALENTINE    OTEL

in the amplitude of leaning wheat.
that sky of untouchable workings

*watch for wind on overpass.*

blood-spots in the grass.
hot-pink poppies fret in the ditch, my arms
in the rupture of air

ninety-mile-an-hour fracas. I see catfish
in the culvert-water, semis dragging their outlines

and the sound. the wind. his shirt rising like a sail

# Broken Engagement

The plan was to meet
for an apricot danish
or two and a pot
of tea on the sidewalk

before noon. It's before
noon and the pavement
is limp with rain. I
step over someone's plastic

fork, cracked tines
like blunt thumbs.
This won't do.
Your marmalade arms,

your hair in its silver clip.
Nothing where your eyes
should be. And still
I stand here with the fork.

Thumbs broken off.
In all this rain.

# Damage

she decided those years had been water vapor,
condensed, then ruptured
into an updraft,
the mad air ascending,
the vertical spin
flicking like a bullwhip over a field

an inkling, a shimmying
spine of wind

that's what it was like, she said,
volatile conditions

the air rolling horizontally
like a pencil,
clouds the color of asphalt and moss,
a disturbance first under the skin, then
sibilance in the leaves,
crescendo,
ascent

a colossal vessel of air
assembling, lifting off like spun smoke,
the invisible suddenly utterly there,
shapely, voracious

rising to wreckage:
metal, shingles, his things, hers,
glass and laceration—

you do what it takes to keep yourself whole

in Andover the sirens fail,
homes turn to shrapnel, roofs tear off
like flimsy lids, rooms empty
into the sky

the Golden Spur Mobile Home Park
flattened, gone, a sink in the street, a nightstand
with its shot of vodka

she said she'd heard that coins fuse in pockets,
that potatoes bake where they lie
in the earth     cows fly by screaming

in springtime the warm sweet hours
between noon and the first star
are most unstable     a car hovers
three feet over the ground in Wichita

then it's gone

garage doors sail the streets
like sheets of paper, a woman sits
in a ditch beside a tractor

gathers herself, her watch
gone, and her shoes

the tree at her feet blown to kindling

she swears before it spent itself
it turned scarlet—

an elongated seething heart, or a mouth
devouring a nursery of geraniums

they don't touch down you know, she said,
they take everything with them

# Accident

*for Jon Lobeck, 1963–1995*

The yard vanishes, thickens
with shadows and leaves that drift
against the fence.

A flurry of grass as the wind picks up
and time comes undone. Last week

a field of withering pumpkins, and snow.
Birds over the freeway wrinkling the sky.
Wind-current of ash. The trip home.

And the boy in his small dark suit
brings a drawing of a bird which he lays
on his father's hands.

Later, outside, more snow.
A few flakes sparkling on his shoes.

An accident that alters everything,
though time passes as before, the light

falling, then sprung, audacious.
People laugh in the streets, buy groceries
and magazines. We go on,

our pettiness and courage like wrong colors.

I walk the next day over leaf-stains
through rain, I am not ready
for the umbrella that opens head-on

as if it had been aimed, point-blank
at close range, someone laughing behind its abrupt
blooming. Combustion of color. A shot.

# Missing

Flash of swift light. The wicker sides of their basket
ignite as they turn to hurry the child. On a city street.
A county park. Beech leaves like a shock of mirrors.
A hawk flies into the sun, comes apart. The child
scatters quietly over the ground. They intended to tell her
how much she was loved, that her hands were the only
sound — But suddenly there is no sound. They watch
a small gash in one of the clouds. The world is finished
with them, drops its sky to the ground. Their bodies reel
like late-summer seeds. Aberrant kites. There is no one,
nothing left to see. There are feathers. There is ash.

# *Witness*

Years later, in another country
    They wake to colored birds

Rising from their eyes
    From eating leaves in the forest—

Hunger that turned their mouths to air

Sometimes what they see breaks
    Into prisms of light

Sometimes they remember

Fires stoked with photographs. Visual evidence
    Shedding the world. A child

Hurled by the ankles, his head collapsing against a tree

They can't see

They think maybe it was the dirt—
    The smoke emptying their eyes

Maybe the corpses, the mines along the path

Months without dreams, or the nightmares
       Better than waking

Fieldwork, abrasive sun
       And the hunger

Everything changed into something else

Sometimes it lasts for months — a seeing through water

Again the man who sold cloth. He said the statue of the Buddha
       Wept in the temple

They remember also what they did not see

Fear brings it sometimes, the vanishing. The vacant marketplace
       A tree like the one where a cousin hung

The necklace of rope —

A daughter broken in a field

Her mother watches her soul lift, sees
       An angel rising into the sun

Other times shadows — a man's leg
       Behind a shed, a face, the shape of a hand

Passing before their eyes. Sometimes they wake to their lives
In other places. Sometimes what they see

Is a flock of birds, a column of smoke, moments of light now and then
Like a brief concentration of stars

# Betrayal

It's how we live, our ungainly love.
Strange tree. How we must look
to the branches, the wind, the split second
of moonlight through which we plunge

again and again. This foraging. But we don't want to
see it, the wild-weed lashes, the cheekbones
angled like shelves. How things become lost.
We betray ourselves, topple. Are discarded.

And the hardest place to look is always the dark spot
in the ditchwater that might be a glove
or something drowned with its eyes open.

# The Lovers

turn frail in the afterlight.
They wonder what they will eat
now that the world is no longer lush.

They drift
where wheat once ruffled and shone,

find a cob of corn and examine its blackening,
collapsing teeth.

Peripheral vision is all they have.

They turn ashen and narrow where a stream
had been,

their voices tear off in the wind.

After a time they feel their transparence, are shocked
at how they can see into bone and through

walls. Their shirts hang in ribbons, float behind them
like smoke.

They leave no fingerprints on what they touch,
no trace in the strange rubble-world
of anything they had loved.

# PART FOUR

# At the Gate

*Sentiment without action is the ruin of the soul.*

EDWARD ABBEY

You're not there
as you are, each hour, in life. On the pavement is rock cress and glass,
*manzanilla*

discarded, the blossoms
collapsing, and the cut stems: glittering trash. The mattress truck
passes. Bus exhaust.

My eyes rebuild the groves
of rubber, bamboo scaffolding, the beggar holding out his glass eye,
     asking me
something.

There are gates in this landscape. One is white stone
with the names of the dead carved deep. It's all in Hebrew, the light here
     burns, there are bushes
of blood in the sand. I am touching the fine groove

of a name or a date, a reason
for this lonely marker. I am thinking of you, even then; wishing you
     would lay me down
in the dust. No words,

no relief. This gate is made of iron, black,
and edging a stony yard. I have wanted to show you, there are angels
and asps here. Wings and tongues. In the dream

I don't mind the sadness of this,
that you stand in the yard behind it, and I in the street among
        overturned cars, fire
billowing from windows.

There's a gate that swings on a screaming hinge.
The sound pains and arouses us, we who've been standing like this
        all night
with the city watching.

We meet to touch, knowing we're watched
though our fingers and tongues have been taken away — some kind
        of exchange
for the gift of our sight. Or a price for our hesitation.

# Blue Thorn

The most dangerous thing is to let someone ignite within us

My husband hung bunches of holly last night—smooth spiked leaves,
polished clots. He's not yet noticed where my eyes have been,
where they go

*the conditions are, I'm afraid to say, very secret*

Though you've figured it out, by mistake, or by instinct or paying
        attention.
For myself I desire some kind of illusion,
an improbable balance

*cinco minutos más tarde no existías*

And the holly is distracting, how the leaves
can wound. I run my hand along a low hedge while we walk

*the compulsion to tell, to leave records*

There have been too many conversations.
We have our opinions, our bleak and beautiful scars. We long, and can
        talk for hours
and say nothing that will matter

There are decisions that have been made, though we cannot be content
with them. I dream of someone I'm in love with, wake

guilty. Climb up from drifts of snow

*I just want to eat those potatoes with onions that are waiting for us*
*upstairs on the fire*

I want back the hunger of adolescence. Even the deceit
we thought we might not survive.
He will marry in three weeks

*the taste lies between burn and nightmare*

I've not let go, though I keep moving

Sleep has begun to worry me so I do it less often. I pace
while he breathes in the other dark

what I call *I* is not even a body

That register of things that happen.
His voice in the stairwell, my face in your hands

Loving to distraction. There's no time, no way, to sit through
            conversations of weather
or other people's children. We know the escape of it
is a drug. We want it more than water nonetheless, more than sleep

*nothing abstract. something about milk and warmth*

What we thought we could be happy with

What I want is that hunger—
the languages indecipherable, wind

on the lawn of the Palace Museum, wind lifting my skirts.
The guards patrolling with their lights.
So many constellations, we had to make love everywhere

*I wonder, what do I associate you with?*

In the morning I duck beneath the holly hanging from the overhead
        light.
I stand at the sink and think how he's tried, in his way, to please me,
        and how
I will not be pleased. I have been giving away my clothes, words

*sur mes cahiers d'écolier, sur les arbres, sur la neige.* Éluard writes
of *appétits machinaux et danses détraquées* —

Repetition through the years. Such *lourdes folies errantes.*

*who was asking the questions?*

Rococo, the edge of the mind

                      ᕁ

On the news they tell of a Midwestern blizzard, and I walk through those
silent padded streets. I go for groceries in my grandmother's fur and
        the walk

is exhausting, the silence and solitude. The fur pushes me down into
        the snow,
touches my neck and wrists and there are blue halos around the
        streetlamps

there are teeth glittering under the eaves. I remember the story of a
    great-uncle
who lost his way on the prairie in a snowstorm. He was drunk, drove
    the car

off the road into a soft white ditch, started walking into the white

These things are not stories. They happen

                              ⌒

And my mother, trying to survive the Dakota sky, her father, the foxes
    in the corncribs,
geese hanging by their stretched necks. Dank heat of horses and barns.
Later trying to do without them

                              ⌒

You want to know why I hold you off? You all want to know this —
what happened in the shut rooms, on the brown or blue sofa

Certain things. The holly. The ache to sleep in a wooden room
in a place where no one waits for me. A place to slip into and be noticed
then forgotten

I don't fall in love so much as succumb to attention; this need to be
    wanted.
I'm on good behavior in the public halls where you look for me.
No tantrums. No real cruelty

*no me importunes ahora.*
*no vengas ahora con recuerdos*

I only love with abandon those who cannot contain me

I want to be alone, but worry I'll miss something. So I've tried
to be married, want children

But I recognize nothing

Can't pull the blue thorn from my throat

I also love a woman

*fog on your eyes without a light*

Ice massed in shards at the edge of a lake. I smell burning

remember a wolf in the snow. I am giving away pieces of my *life*—
the fine stones and bits of shell

And he'll weary. He knows what I am.
Later I'll only want a new stranger, a new set of obsessions, eyes
            telling me
*I cannot live without you*

*like a satellite crazed with a planet*

The most dangerous thing is to be caught like this

*when I look at you I feel the world's hunger*

A voice in the next room, heavy, low,
whispering into the phone

*there's this guttural voice coming out of your eyes*

Talk of love on the Spanish Steps
where a man rolls, barechested, on shattered glass

# Conversation

my brother, my spouse, my cousin's ex
grow tense. the conversation turns
then, to the thing they most fear

(the sky full of holes; punched-in
clouds and hiddenness). they insist on
the truth. they must know, they say,

The Truth. this of course pertains to fidelity.
sexual. they insist there is no way to live
with the unknown. intolerable

to have to wonder where she spread her legs
and who might have been there for it.
(did she moan? speak? into whose mouth?

just *how* was she touched?) I mention that
the mountain ash in the backyard is nearly
dead (a wildness is crowding the room—

heat and fists). someone pounded a nail
into its trunk and this spring it didn't survive.
they are livid. they ask

what that has to do with anything.

# A Few Words on Penis Envy

I cannot believe you
      believed this, did you
      perhaps spend multiple boyhood hours
wishing for a delicate slit

of your own? Did you crave
      such a private inside
      space, something more subtle
than your own public

divining rod, twitching
      with swollen sexual weather,
      the pubic intonations
suddenly grown

obvious? Could it be, Sig,
      you so wanted a cunt
      with its quiet serious strength
that you could not sleep

and so one night fashioned
      this curious notion, this cockeyed
      conceit that dangles, silly,
in our hands?

# First Child

As the floor tilts, the hanging lamp
dangles at an odd slant toward the kitchen's
star-of-Bethlehem walls

and I
know the stillness, the belligerent pace, the public shadows
on our lawn

and the way she stood at the edge of the orchard, transparent
in her nightdress as the bus crept up the drive.
The kids yucked it up then, all through the day,
about the nipples she'd flashed at them again,
the half-baked mama who took her babies to bed
when it stormed, who sent her gentle husband away
for neglecting the foxglove and her Indian magic crab.

We were told to be able and fluid, though two of us
were born gaunt. I grew my hair long, spent hours at Labyrinth,
and locked the door to the playhouse, though always she found
a way in. Once in a fit of temper she cut my hair
with a knife, wrapped the thicker end in ribbon, and
hung it from the freezer door with a blue hook magnet.
The cat found her finally under the basement steps

and I
have walked a long way to avoid that script, the smell of her
like quince.

Having made it this far
south, I find I miss the snow,
the kitchen, the sudden severity of Christmas.

# Self-Portrait Diptych

The eyes aren't right. The mind
unnerved by quick translations,
and the words I choose give this away.

Elusive, fluid, chaotic, and rinsed.

Contentious, intricate, fractious.

Stubborn, ancient,
and vain.
Cassava fields and Trinidad,
abrasions, damask,

succulents, shame, incantation.

I want Istanbul, Persia, mosaic pools.
Blue-green undertow, black

pearls. Anemone. Washed stones.
The sea, mountain avens, Tibet.

Glass and its particulars.
The possibilities of light.

Reflection and mirror and moon,

tenuous fissure,
nightfall-blue.

Conceit of diamonds, insinuation,
thistle, and scarlet brocade.

Tantrums, tourmaline,
whitewash, and frost.

Lemon trees, sutures, Marrakech.

Petroglyphs. Lapis.

Arctic melon.
Indigo fig.

⌒

I was happy, truly happy, only twice.

Once on the moors. Tintagel like a dark gem,
seacaves and tidepools
and myself, soaring from the rocks.

Myself as seafoam, green waves.
Gorse growing wild where I died.

In Rome I worshiped Neptune's piazza,
the dizzying light, and his dragons, seacreatures,
immaculate thighs.

A boy followed me, eyes like black stones.
I was not the same after that,

not the same.

Now this is the story.
The book of glass.

# April

spring blurs the underbrush, an oak
exhales, discards its bark.
the woods are a mess.

᚜

still there's bounty in it.
this time of year things move
from sheer to tender.

the rivers' syllabics and cuttings
of light. a caress pressing forth.

surfaces still touched
with chill, still cautious, but softening.

᚜

I know this, the woods' pulse.
bracken and roots, the collapse
of sparrows' nests, fallen limbs,

evidence of how it is.
and the earthsmells lifting like subterfuge,
like tactile steam

from the loam and rot. I'm thankful
now for the elms, for bristling water.
how thaw throws off the ice

and swallows it. how things lift
toward flush and bulk.
the wind brightening and loose.

I remember everything suddenly,
your wrists in sunshine,

the leaves arriving like anthems.

ᢣ

old weather flickers, still raw
some moments, still here, but easier.
so wonder comes back

with a grassy rush. a wren flirts
in the new-sprung and settled mesh.
how intricate. how foolish and dear

to believe each time that
we've come upon something new.

# Prayer

*I love you so I swear I do adore you*
TRISTAN TZARA

From the wreck and tangle of the past moon the past
moment every minute since this thirst began,
       I lean
             I stumble toward you hoping
      you've not turned away yet

        hoping there might be something here
      to hold your falling eyes, tack your feet
      to the floor

             If I could escape my head
for one day
        and come to you as tongue, as open mouth proud
        hunger and thighs, as fingernail and footsole

lapis and emerald

If I could come to you
        without my voice pulling words
        around the sound
but just carry you with me
              to the water
        and walk our bodies in until our mouths are under-

neath us and making *O*s, marking us
with sucking, octopus and leech

If I could I would leave
the flimsy skin of my intellect on the sand

like a towel, a blouse, to change shape and texture
into wind

# what we are

detritus, windburn, a lazy eye. filament, flux,
and implication. overabundance

of white, lamentation

duplicity laying claim. delirium
and water. deer soughing past

a woodpile. flicker of tongues, old eyes.
ice. a long moan running down the shore.

the ache and threat of want, the possibility of being ruined
by a breath. a glance.

a quick wind, a slamming door.

the wrong eyes at the window.

white birch. the moon's stain. what wasn't said
but took root nonetheless. that look you have when you shake off sleep
        and come back to me
(your mind working hard to unfold, *quickly, quickly*).

desire and stupor. history. this.
tracks through snow, leading out.

# Notes

STILL LIFE

"Still Life" comes from Paul Strand's photograph *Still Life, Pear and Bowls* (Twin Lakes, Connecticut, 1916). Märchen is German for folktale or fairy story.

HOOP SNAKE

The line "the unheard melodies and those that catch" is adapted from Keats.

RED TIDE

From *American Heritage Dictionary of the English Language:* red tide— "A bloom of dinoflagellates that causes reddish discoloration of coastal ocean waters. Certain dinoflagellates of the genus *Gonyamlax* produce toxins that kill fish and contaminate shellfish."

CHIROPTERA

Chiroptera is an order of flying mammals; in this poem, bats.

THOUGHT

*La pensée se fait dans la bouche:* Thought takes place in the mouth.

UNCERTAIN GRACE

The poem and title come from Sebastião Salgado's photography exhibit *An Uncertain Grace: Photographs by Sebastião Salgado,* Corcoran Gallery of Art, Washington, D.C., January through March 1992.

AJABU

This poem is based on an event experienced by my cousin and her husband while they were working in Kenya from 1990 to 1991.

### BAUDELAIRE TO HIS MOTHER

This poem was inspired by a collection of Charles Baudelaire's letters.

### MOUNT PLEASANT HYDRANGEA

Mount Pleasant is a neighborhood located on the east side of the Washington, D.C., National Zoo.

### INTARSIA

Intarsia is a type of mosaic developed in fifteenth-century Italy, in which a veneer is inlaid with various colors and types of wood, forming an ornate pattern or picture.

### AFTER THE CRAZY MOUNTAINS

Dedicated to Jan Keessen and Kirsten Finstad. An Apache tear is a type of stone.

### DAMAGE

This poem includes information adapted from a *National Geographic* presentation, "Twister!"

### WITNESS

Dedicated to Carolyn Forché.

### BLUE THORN

Prompted by Kate Chopin's *The Awakening.* Certain italicized lines are borrowed/adapted from the work of a friend, Alfredo Pérez, and used with his permission.

> *cinco minutos más tarde no existías:* five minutes later you no longer existed

*sur mes cahiers d'écolier, sur les arbres, sur la neige:* on my school notebooks, on the trees, on the snow

*appétits machinaux et danses détraquées:* mechanical appetites and uncontrolled dances

*lourdes folies errantes:* heavy wandering madnesses

*no me importunes ahora:* don't interrupt me now

*no vengas ahora con recuerdos:* don't come now with memories

# About the Author

Rebecca Liv Wee teaches creative writing in the English Department at Augustana College in Rock Island, Illinois. In 1992 she received her MFA in poetry from George Mason University in Fairfax, Virginia, where she studied for three years with Carolyn Forché, C.K. Williams, Susan Tichy, Peter Klappert, and others. She is the recipient of seven previous poetry prizes and awards including a 1994–95 grant from the Minnesota State Arts Board. During her graduate studies she served as poetry editor for *So to Speak,* GMU's women's literary arts journal, and as editorial assistant to Carolyn Forché on her 1993 anthology, *Against Forgetting: Twentieth-Century Poetry of Witness.* Wee's poems have appeared in *The Iowa Review, Phoebe, Ploughshares, The Plum Review, Rag Mag, The Sonora Review,* and elsewhere.

The Chinese character for poetry is made up of two parts: "word" and "temple."
It also serves as pressmark for Copper Canyon Press.

Founded in 1972, Copper Canyon Press remains dedicated to publishing poetry
exclusively, from Nobel laureates to new and emerging authors. The press
thrives with the generous patronage of readers, writers, booksellers, librarians,
teachers, students, and funders—everyone who shares the conviction
that poetry invigorates the language and sharpens
our appreciation of the world.

PUBLISHER'S CIRCLE

Allen Foundation for the Arts
Elliott Bay Book Company
Mimi Gardner Gates
Jaech Family Fund
Lannan Foundation
Rhoady and Jeanne Marie Lee
Lila Wallace–Reader's Digest Fund
National Endowment for the Arts
Port Townsend Paper Company
U.S.–Mexico Fund for Culture
Emily Warn and Daj Oberg
Washington State Arts Commission
The Witter Bynner Foundation
Charles and Barbara Wright

*For information and catalogs:*

COPPER CANYON PRESS
Post Office Box 271
Port Townsend, Washington 98368
360/385-4925
poetry@coppercanyonpress.org
www.coppercanyonpress.org

The font used is Perpetua, designed by Eric Gill. Gill worked as a stonecutter and engraver. These influences may be seen in the flat, beaked terminals on letters like the *y* and in the elegance of the capital letters. Despite an echo of chisel on stone, Perpetua has a delicate vulnerability. Book design and composition by Valerie Brewster, Scribe Typography. Printed on archival-quality Glatfelter Author's Text by McNaughton & Gunn, Inc.

CPSIA information can be obtained
at www.ICGtesting.com
Printed in the USA
JSHW020326230123
36414JS00001B/3

9 781556 591549